SOMETHING IN THE WOODS
is taking people...
Stephen Young

Something in the Woods is taking people.

Something unknown that we cannot define; something that others have had the misfortune to encounter.

People snatched soundlessly, never to be seen again. Or returned; dead.

A strange and highly unusual predator. Highly intelligent. Very successful. And able to overpower someone in an instant.

This is a puzzle. An often deadly one.

Here follows some very troubling and disturbing accounts....

Table of Contents

Introduction

Fatal accidents can happen very easily to even the most experienced climbers, and in the wilderness, hikers can get lost in an instant. A couple of wrong turns and they can be lost immediately. A slip on a rock or a trip near a crevice and death or serious accidents can come quickly.

Falling into a creek or down between a pile of rocks, a body; dead or injured, can be hidden from search parties quite easily. However, with highly trained tracker dogs and heat seeking infra-red equipment to detect a person's body heat, the mystery often remains as to why people are not found, or are found in the most unusual of circumstances.

Natural predators can lurk in the wilderness; bears, cougars, and occasionally a hiker will be victim to these wild animals. They feed where they kill, or drag their bloody victim to a nearby lair; they leave a trail that is obvious to searchers.

However, the victims in this book show no evidence of an animal attack.

For these victims, there is no logical explanation....only enigma and many questions...

Something in the Woods is taking people....

People taken; sometimes returned, but never the same again.

Chapter One:
The Disappeared

As of writing this in June 2014, after days of thorough ground and air searches, rescuers still haven't been able to locate a fire-fighter and paramedic who disappeared while on an off-duty hiking trip with a friend in the Los Padres National Forest, Arizona.

Fit and athletic Mr Herdman had taken off barefoot one evening, chasing his dog when it had started running off from their camp. He hasn't been seen since.

His dog was later seen during the subsequent search. Search dogs were used in the area where Herdman's footprints were found, but it seems the tracker dogs have not been able to trace his scent any further than the immediate area he was last seen in.

(Author Update: Tragically, his body has since been found. After a substantive search that lasted two weeks, involving constant aerial and ground searches, using hundreds of SAR teams and volunteers, K9's, and heat-seeking equipment, he was found deceased lying on a steep ascent approximately 2,000 feet from where he had last been seen.

He'd suffered blunt force trauma. It was determined that he'd fallen, though when this occurred can't be determined beyond "a few days."

He was found in the same area in which searchers had been looking for him, night and day, for the last fourteen days.

Why was his scent not able to be picked up? How had it just stopped?

Why was he not seen? Though much of the area is dense in vegetation, he was only partially covered by brush and clearly visible on a rock surface.

How could he have been there all that time?

If he hadn't been there for that duration, where had he been?

"What's the chances someone barefoot, at night, would scale a mountain of 1200 feet?" said the Sheriff.

As to why he'd been attempting to climb a rock edge, the investigating Sheriff commented, "I'm not sure we'll get an answer."

The Sheriff stated that he did not appear to have been trapped and that he appeared to be lying over the ground.

It was then stated that the area where he'd been found had *not* been searched; yet we know over 50 square miles *had* been searched? It also still doesn't explain how the tracker dogs had not picked up a scent to lead them to where his body was located.

Why had he climbed a cliff? Was he fleeing something?

In July 2012, sixty-six-year-old Michael LeMaitre was the subject of a huge search effort in Alaska that was to last several days.

He'd completed many marathons and was competing in the Seward's Mount race. Last spotted by race organisers approaching the mid point of the race, on a busy main trail, they expected him back at the five kilometre finish shortly after. He was never seen again.

Despite thorough and intensive searching with tracker dogs, they could find no trace of him and no scent to follow. Thermal imaging equipment searched for signals of his body, yet none could be found.

Hundreds of volunteers took to the area, searching every possible crevice for over ten days.

How could he disappear in so small a spot they all wondered, running a planned round route of just 5k and surrounded by other runners? They were mystified by finding absolutely no trace of him.

He disappeared without trace. Every crevice was searched. He left no scent to track.

It's almost as though he was plucked into the air. He certainly wasn't on the ground anymore...

* * *

In July 2006, student Aju Iroaga was standing alone on a country road just by Lake Superior, having stormed off-site of a tree planting project.

He'd been told to re-do the trees he'd just planted and he was angry. He'd already re-done his work once, and he was exhausted. Now he was stuck there, in the middle of the forest, several kilometres from the company base. He'd been told if he was quitting, he'd have to wait for the team to finish and then he would be taken back to the base to get his belongings and leave.

He waited for nearly four hours, just standing there, and was last noticed still there at about quarter to four in the afternoon. At 6pm when the team finished however, he had disappeared.

Concerned, the supervisors and team looked around for him, two of them even staying there that night in case he turned up.

Police officers arrived at about 11 pm, and at dawn they began their search with helicopters and K9 units to pick up the students trail. However, the dogs could find no scent of him.

The police's original theory was that he'd decided to walk through the wilderness to the camp. They had nothing else to go on; but no footprints or scent to track either.

He was never seen again.

At one stage, the Ontario Police suggested that because he was a fit young man, he may have run an access road the length of over *60km* to the Trans Canada Highway to hitch a ride.

Despite how fit he was it seems a highly unlikely theory.

A website put together by the heartbroken family says, "That there is no evidence of foul play, and no evidence that he walked off, leaves an unacceptable mystery. People simply do not vanish."

The co-owner of the company he was there working for was quoted as saying, "He was certainly strong enough, both in will and physically to be able to take care of himself."

Where did he go? And what did he meet that was stronger than him?

* * *

In June 2013, the Reiger family from Oklahoma were on vacation in Ecuador. The family decided to take a short hike from their hotel, along a scenic trail. At some point along the hike, the two boys ran on ahead but only one of them returned.

The elder son it seemed had disappeared into thin air. The boys were close to each other on the hike, separated only momentarily when the elder had vanished.

"The really strange thing about it is," his father told newspapers, "that whatever happened to him was in the space of five minutes; we were right behind him. You couldn't get lost. The whole of the trail is visible. If he was hurt, he would have been seen."

Searchers could not seem to locate the boy's tracks, and indeed stated that they didn't detect any other tracks in the boy's vicinity either. No-one heard him shout or scream, no sounds of any thrashing in the undergrowth or of a fall, no blood, no scent.

Army troops were called in and the Soldiers rappelled down the ravines, tracker dogs, fire-fighters, and volunteers from the village below joined in.

Some have suggested, given that they could not find a body in the ravines, and that they couldn't detect his scent, that the most logical thing that could have happened was that he was suddenly 'lifted' from the ground by something. It's as though he was somehow 'disappeared' into invisibility.

"I could see; I was there. I don't know why they didn't find him. He would have been seen. I cannot come up with a scenario that makes any sense. Nothing makes any sense," says his Father.

* * *

'A hiker's disappearance adds to hundreds of others,' wrote an Oregon newspaper in 2013.

They'd discovered that an astonishing figure of two hundred and forty people were recorded as missing after going into the Oregon wilderness since the late nineties.

Highlighting just two of the cases, they related how a former member of the United States Coast Guards had disappeared in the Willamette National Forest in 2012.

His profession had depended on him being extremely fit and athletic, and he kept up his level of fitness after leaving with frequent hikes and cycling. However, once he entered the national park he was never seen again. Nor were any of his belongings, including an inflatable raft and his cell-phone. Bodies will sadly succumb to the elements, but other things are more durable; they don't decompose. They weren't found either though.

Jake's mother told the reporter, "There's a mystery here. Both were experienced. Two grown men can't simply disappear."

She was referring to six years prior to this, when a professor of mathematics at Oregon University, Dr Xu, went hiking near the spot where her son Jake had been. No sign of him has been seen either.

The search had covered one hundred miles of the forest using tracker dogs and heat seeking equipment. For a while they followed footprints that were thought to be his, but the trail suddenly stopped.

How can a trail suddenly stop and yet there be no explanation as to where he had gone from there?

Chapter Two:
Hunting for Explanations. UFO and Alien Involvement?

In 2002, the strange story of what happened to Todd Sees began to circulate. Could it really be true what was being said?

Early in the morning on August 4th, Todd left his rural home in Northumberland, Pennsylvania to go up into the nearby mountain to do some deer scouting, prior to the season starting. As he left, he told his family he would be home by midday.

When he didn't return his concerned wife alerted authorities, knowing it was completely out of character for him not to return as he'd said he would.

By 2pm, a search party had been organized. The State police and a couple hundred local volunteers began to search for him. Quickly they discovered his four-wheeler at the top of the mountain, but search dogs could find no scent to go on.

The search carried on for two days, from top to bottom of the mountainous area.

On the second day a break came; something was seen in a thick brush area beside a pond, very close to the family home. The search party spent half an hour hacking at the brush to get to it. What they found was Todd Sees' body, virtually naked. He was wearing just his underwear. When he'd left two days before, he'd been fully dressed in outdoor clothing and boots.

His body was not bloated; it was emaciated. Immediately there were concerns. That would not be the usual condition to find a body in.

It got stranger. Though many locals claimed afterward there was nothing unusual about the incident, others, including Emmy award winning investigative journalist Linda Molten Howe, and Peter Davenport of the National UFO Reporting Centre, believed there was a lot more to the case. They pointed to the fact that the area had been previously searched, and yet the tracker dogs had not been able to pick up his scent at all. Why?

This led to speculation that his body could not have been there when the area was searched, but was perhaps placed there later.

His body was found in a thickly forested spot, so difficult to access that it led many to believe he could not have gone there voluntarily, by his own volition, if the searchers themselves had to hack their way into it to retrieve him.

But who or what had taken him in there if it was such a difficult area to get to?

Even odder, one of his missing boots was later found; high up in a tree a mile from where his vehicle was found, and no-where near his body. People wanted to know how the boot could have got up there.

There were claims that upon the discovery of his body, the FBI arrived, cordoning off the area and refusing to allow the family access to Todd.

It's implied by researchers including ex-detective Butch Witkowski, that Sees was an unfortunate victim of an alien abduction. Their claims are allegedly back up by reports of sightings by three local farmers of a large bright object just above the power lines, hovering in the area at the time of Sees disappearance.

The official cause of his death was ruled as a cocaine overdose. Those close to him state he was not a drug taker.

* * *

A case as strange as that of Todd Sees happened in the U.K. in 1980. Zygmunt Adamski disappeared from Todmorden in the rural county of Yorkshire on June 6, 1980 after leaving his house.

Five days later his body was located on the top of a coal pile in a coal mine.

The police attended the scene, where on examination they found burn marks on the man's shoulders and neck, and a strange green ointment covering the wounds. The ointment was never able to be scientifically identified.

His clothes were clean despite him having been missing for five days, although his jacket had been buttoned up incorrectly and his shirt was missing. There were no footprints in the coal.

The Mine Company's son was the last person in the area, but he'd been there before midday. He had seen no body on a coal pile. It appeared to have been put there after that time.

The pathologist ruled that his death had occurred between eleven and one pm of that day, but the burns on his body were determined to have occurred two days before his death.

He stated, "What led to his death couldn't be answered," but he ruled that the man had died of a heart attack due to shock or fright. His face had been contorted with fear.

The case was never solved any further than that, but oddly enough a few months after finding the man's body there, one of the policemen, Alan Godfrey, was on a night shift and claimed to have experienced an unnerving incident himself.

Searching for some missing cows, he claimed that he saw a strange large object in front of him in the road, hovering above the ground.

He tried to radio colleagues, but his radio went dead. Frightened, he remained in the car.

He was later to realise that over half an hour had passed that he couldn't account for, and he found that the soles of his boots were split wide open, looking to him as though he'd been dragged along the ground.

That same night other policemen independently called into headquarters with alarming reports of seeing bright lights descending into the valley, and a driver also called the police.

The cows were later discovered in a field which had been previously empty and the entrance gate to it was locked. The ground was muddy, but there were no prints from the cows. Like the man, it was as though they too had literally been dropped there.

The policeman himself was so disturbed by his experience that he underwent hypno-regression, in search of answers about what could have happened to him in the missing half an hour.

Under a state of hypnosis he began to describe being in a room with a black-robed, bearded man with a biblical appearance, accompanied by a huge black dog and other, smaller 'creatures' that were the size of five year olds and had robotic movements.

* * *

In 1992, *Napa Valley Register* interviewed young film maker Jake Polania regarding his plan to make a film about an incident that occurred in Flagstaff, Arizona. According to Polania, four young friends were on their return from a camping trip when somehow three of them, along with a farm hand, were found dead on a ranch. The fourth friend, along with the owner of the farm were missing.

The deaths were never solved. The fourth camper and the owner were never found. The bodies of the dead campers had strange marks on their necks and backs, but there was no blood at the scene. The local sheriffs spent two weeks searching for the missing men but found no clues.

* * *

Lecturer on paranormal and esoteric matters, Guy Tarade mentions a mysterious incident that most who heard about attributed it to a UFO abduction, though there were no reports of any witnesses to one being seen in the area at the time.

According to Miami police reports, in 1952 a Mr Tom Brook, his wife, and their 11 year-old son had been visiting friends thirty kilometres away from Miami, and had left just before midnight to drive back home.

Local law enforcement officers came across their empty car; the headlights ablaze and the doors open, just seven miles from their friend's home. Mrs. Brooke's handbag was found in the back seat, the money still in it.

The officers traced the family's footprints to a meadow at the edge of the roadside, but they abruptly stopped after a few dozen steps.

According to reports available, no trace of them was ever found.

Chapter Three:
Invisible Assailants?

The oldest journal still in publication, The Scots Magazine, first issued in 1739, wrote of a very strange incident that occurred in 1761.

Five women were returning from collecting wood near Ventimiglia in northern Italy, when suddenly one of them cried out and dropped to the ground, dead. Her friends were terrified by what they saw.

Her clothes and even her shoes were apparently torn into shreds and scattered all around her. Her wounds were horrific; her skull was visible, her intestines hanging out, and most of her internal organs ruptured. Her femur had been torn from its socket and the flesh of her hip and thigh torn off.

The account was recorded in the French Academy of Sciences by Dr M. Morand. He wrote that there was no blood at the scene, nor any sign of her missing flesh.

***

Researchers John Mitchell and Robert Rickard wrote of an account from the famous explorer James Alan Rennie and his friend, who were in the remote wilderness of northern Canada in 1924. According to them, as they made their way across a frozen lake they encountered something that chilled them to the very core.

Tracks were appearing in front of them, coming toward them yet no creature was making them; there was nothing there except the recurring tracks coming closer. Then suddenly, something impacted against Rennie, then ventured on at great speed, its tracks still being made as the invisible entity made its way across the lake.

The explorer recorded in his published journal, "There was no animal, no sign of any life at all to account for them."

***

A few decades ago in the field of Ufology and Cryptozoology there began a growing field of thought that pointed to the possibility of invisible 'intelligences' on a grand scale.

Known as 'Atmospheric beings,' they're a theory of what one would think impossible. Sky-bound entities that roam the skies in silence, visible only by the use of infra-red but always there.

They remain one of the most fascinating of mysteries that fall somewhere within the Cryptozoology and Ufology fields, with a leaning toward the esoteric too.

Their origins unknown and their intentions possibly sinister.

We don't know what they are, but they are there none the less, and these things appear to be alive. Organic creatures of some sort.

Large, voracious, invisible to the naked eye; these undetectable predators could take people without seeing them coming.

This is what Navy veteran Trevor Constable believed, dedicating twenty years to studying them. The idea that these morphic beasts he could capture with the use of infra-red cameras, that dwelt within the atmosphere of the earth, were monsters that only increased their density while in search of food; their food source being humans.

He blamed the accounts of livestock disappearances, mutilations, and indeed human mutilation cases, on these soaring predatory entities, along with the constant stream of people going missing every year.

In the 1950's he captured up to 100 images on film while out in places such as the Yucca Valley and the Mojave Desert; some showed dark objects, others showed shadowed dense beings looking like living cells. Others took the form of UFO's. All were framed by the landscape, enabling their size to be scaled in comparison to natural features. They were frighteningly big.

For the first time they were being captured by infra-red, but for years reports have surfaced of strange creatures inhabiting the skies above us. Atmospheric beasts, or atmospheric life-forms, with bodies that are able to adjust their density from the almost immaterial and invisible to a more solid form; actual life-forms with an intelligence. Morphing, shape-shifting, and attacking.

He wasn't the only one to capture their images. According to Rense magazine, photographer Michael White was filming the night sky when he noticed an odd-looking dark cloud which remained stationary and did not move at all for at least thirty minutes, before then suddenly disappearing.

It wasn't until he later developed the images he'd photographed that he saw there was some kind of entity there; a mysterious object that looked like it had been *rippling*. Though to the naked eye it appeared solid, in the pictures there were shadows of light and fibrous looking shapes.

They roam the skies in silence; invisible, but always there. Shimmering predators that shift in density as they swoop down to attack.

Prior to both of these investigators, the late Ivan Sanderson was a proponent of the theory.

If this sounds too fantastical to believe, perhaps it should be noted that in 1949, the US Air force made a revealing official statement that, "the possible existence of some sort of strange 'ET' animals has been considered, as many of the 'objects' (seen in the Sky) act more like animals than anything else."

Then came some startling news. In 2013, The Telegraph Newspaper had the headline 'Aliens exist and have been found living high up in the sky.' University of Sheffield scientists had found organisms living up in the atmosphere. This they said could possibly be the first real proof that life had come from space to earth.

The article points out that this is not the first time organisms have been found; the skies are thought to be full of life.

"Our conclusion is," they said, "life is arriving to Earth from space...life is not restricted to this planet."

Chapter Four:
Malevolent Spirits? The Djinn, Fairies.

"There is something taking these people; something terrible and evil," says Alan Lamers on Dreamlands talk show.

Alan Lamers is a telecoms designer who specialises in creating radio communication systems in remote areas. Contracted to work on the remote Indonesian island of Sulawesi, he found himself in the midst of some very disturbing recurring incidents. He describes in fascinating details these events.

It began he says when he was going to a small village and was told not to wear any coloured clothing; only black or white. Asking why, he was told that people who wore bright coloured clothing could disappear. Though puzzled, he politely complied, more out of cultural respect than any belief in what they were saying, and on arriving at the village destination he saw all of the locals dressed only in black.

As a group, Alan went with several of them into the jungle wilderness. One of his colleagues had not complied with the request and had on a pair of bright coloured socks. When they returned from the jungle that night, his friend started to become violently sick with a very high fever. His body was covered in mysterious scratches. He had not seen anything attacking him. The villagers commented that he was lucky he had not been "taken."

Lamers went on to hear some of the local stories. He spoke to a girl who told him that her cousin and four friends had gone into the jungle for a hike. After a week they had not returned and at great cost she hired a private search party. She went with them, spending a month searching for her cousin and friends.

Finally, they found her cousin; he was severely traumatised however and had no memory of what had happened to him. He was so distressed by whatever had happened to him while missing, that he could not talk for two months. The girl said she believed he had encountered the Djinn. As for his friends; they were never found.

Says Lamers, after interviewing many more locals about their stories, "There is something taking these people. Something terrible and evil. It is one of the strangest and most dangerous places I have ever come across. The locals claimed it is evil spirits, or djinn, snatching away any man who ventured disrespectfully into their terrain."

He finally managed to talk to the boy who'd disappeared and was told by him that he'd been taken by 'little people or creatures,' with black eyes and enormous gaping, grinning mouths. He kept seeing them, but his companions could not. Then they took him to a place filled with animals somewhat like horses or deer.

Although little is known about them in Western countries, The Qur'an refers to the Djinn many times.

In Islamic belief they are thought to be made of a smoke-like yet physical form, and are able to interfere with humans, often to the effect of causing them great harm.

They are mostly thought to be unable to be seen by humans, and are believed to have the power to move at great speed. They have the ability to appear in our world in any form, though often they will look demonic when they fully materialise.

Their domains are naturally remote areas, desert, and mountains. They are thought to be elementals, who can take the form of storms and great winds, and many scholars believe that because of their malevolent nature, they take great pleasure in abducting humans in this guise.

Editor of the *Flying Saucer Review,* Gordon Creighton, expressed the opinion that these elemental beings known to the Islamic world as djinn, could be the culprits in many of the mysterious disappearances of people.

These Arabic beliefs in djinn spirits are aligned to the ancient Celtic beliefs in Fairies. If the idea of Fairies seems a little outlandish, French scientist Jacques Vallees spoke of the parallels that exist between Fairy 'kidnappings' and alleged alien abductions; ranging from seeing strange lights, missing time, and hypnotic mind control.

Fantasy writer Kevin L. O'Brien has significantly researched Celtic and 'Faerie Lore.' 'Faeries' he describes are beings that live communally in the hills, rocks, mountains, or underground.

They use the power of 'glamour;' a power of illusion where they can make people see whatever they wish them to see. They can mislead people in the wilderness by changing the appearance of landmarks, or disguising treacherous ground to make it appear that it's safe to cross.

Faeries have the ability to Shape-shift and transform themselves into any form they choose, similar to the Native American tradition of the Skinwalker.

Sometimes they snatch humans and carry them away, either to be taken forever, or disposed of when finished with. Every seven years the Faeries must make a sacrifice to the devil and give him one of their own, and many old tales describe human captives being given to the devil so that no Faeries will be lost.

Professor DL Ashliman, retired from the University of Petersburg, wrote a paper entitled 'Abducted by Aliens,' in which he quotes an extraordinary story form John Rhys' book, Celtic Folklore. A man in the Isle of Man, (situated between Ireland and England) many years ago suddenly disappeared from his family. He was gone for four years, when one day he suddenly reappeared. He couldn't explain how he had returned, but he told his brothers he'd been living with the fairies.

Obviously skeptical and full of ridicule, the brothers didn't believe him; until he explained that 'the other world' where he had been with the fairies was not far away from them and he'd been able to see what his brothers had been doing every day, though they couldn't see him.

To prove it, he described how the brothers had been collecting wood one afternoon when they'd been so scared by a loud cracking sound in a bush near them that they'd all run back home terrified. His brothers remembered that day well, and knew there was no other way their brother could have known about it. They took his story then as proof.

Perhaps the first study of Fairies was conducted in the 1600's by a Scottish Vicar, Dr Robert Kirk, who compiled accounts of sightings. He believed they were composed of ethereal bodies like clouds, and in a realm somewhere between humans and angels.

Sometimes just their voices could be heard. They could move around in the air and sweep down to snatch things or people away. Other times they materialised like miniature people.

In the 1678, a small book was distributed in England containing the story told by a Dr Moore who claimed that as a young child in Ireland he had been snatched away by the Fairies on more than one occasion. He was relating those events to friends one evening in a remote countryside Pub when they witnessed him violently attacked by something invisible to their eyes and dragged from the Pub.

They quickly went to the local 'Witch' who said he was being held in the woods. She told them that as long as he did not eat anything offered to him by his captors, he would probably return soon unscathed.

He did return, dehydrated and hungry, having found himself alone in the middle of the woods.

In 'Drolls Traditions,' Robert Hunt's book of true stories from Cornwall, England, 1865, he documents a tale one woman gave him. A young boy was out picking flowers in the fields near a wood one evening. He started hearing the most beautiful music coming out of the woods and he walked toward the woods to find out where it was coming from. It seemed to be coming from inside the woods and as he entered it seemed as though the music was in front of him but moving away from him at the same time, almost luring him further to it.

He knew he shouldn't be going further into the woods but the music sounded so beautiful to his ears that he couldn't help but follow it.

Soon he found himself deep inside the woods, and the trees and bushes were thick around him but something invisible was clearing a path for him to walk through, and it seemed almost like night had fallen now, and there were incredibly bright stars filling the sky.

He reached a lake and the music stopped. Feeling tired after his long walk he lay down and fell quickly asleep.

When the search party finally found him several days later, he told his parents that a beautiful woman had taken him into a palace made of gold and crystals of every colour of the rainbow. He had been missing for much longer than one night.

The woman telling the story said she believed it, as did many in a region where witchcraft and paganism have long since existed. She felt that he must have been taken to fairyland after being entranced by them.

In the 1930's The Dublin Press in Ireland had reports of boys sighting groups of fairies and trying to chasing them but unable to catch them as they teasingly jumped through hedges and trees, all the while appearing as glistening and glowing figures, unscathed by the elements they passed through. At moments they appeared to have faces like those of men; hairy and rugged yet they had no ears.

It's said that Iceland is a nation that takes the belief in Faeries so seriously still that to this day they adhere to the principle of not building or disturbing places where they know fairies could dwell, such as boulders and rocky areas. They construct around them, rather than disturb their natural habitat, in respect for them.

Zimbabwe's Mount Inyangani is another mysterious region known for its number of unusual disappearances. *Bulawayo 24* news station on January 12th 2014, reported the search for a missing man 31 year old tourist Zayd Dada, who'd been missing then for over a week.

It seemed again, that in media outlets and on internet sites discussions began revolving around the mythos of the Mountain, of its belief by many as being 'sacred.' People were talking about the mountain that *FATE* Magazine once investigated for its disturbing reputation. The magazine had unearthed the local custom of offering sacrifices in blood to the mountain, in the hope that it would lead to the return of those who had been 'taken.'

Known disappearances there have included two children of a former Government Minister, and a few years later, a young boy Robert Ackhurst. No trace was ever found of any of them, despite extensive searching.

The Magazine however also uncovered several other incidents. Another Government Minister had once become lost there while hiking with two friends. He told of finding themselves wandering without direction in a strange state of disorientation without the normal sensations of thirst or hunger, and most intriguingly of all, as the search party looked for them, the trio spotted them and continually shouted out to them and waved to them but though they could clearly see the search party, the rescuers could not see them.

Another Official of the Government also went missing while walking there. Speaking to a District Assistant, the reporter heard that this man reappeared two days later, in good health but completely unable to recall where he had been or what he had done in the time he was missing.

Mutwa, a Zulu Shaman, has told many of what happened to him while in the hillsides looking for herbs. Suddenly it became cold despite the heat of the day and he was shrouded by bright blue smog that engulfed him. The next thing he knew, he was prostrate on a slab inside a mountainside tunnel, paralysed and unable to escape while grey skinny creatures with long limbs held him captive, his throat burning from sulphuric stench.

Now in 2014 this latest 'victim,' Dada, had been hiking with his wife and two others when they'd stopped for a rest. He continued on aways with the intention of returning to them shortly; but that was the last time he was seen.

Many thorough searches were carried out over the next few days but no sign of him was found.

It was at this stage that traditional tribal healers gathered on the mountain, holding a ritual with the intention of appeasing the spirits of the mountain.

The District Administrator, speaking to the local newspaper was reported as saying, "Mysterious events continue happening."

He said there were many known examples of people who had disappeared there, to be found months or even years later, yet with no ability to describe what happened to them.

In Zayd's case a facebook page was set up appealing for any information, and on one post, a member of the public from the area writes,

"You should consult a witch doctor; I encourage you to; that's the only way you will find him. I'm a Christian but, they will help...'

A Parks spokesperson told reporters at Coastweek news "People are dealing with a situation of the spiritual realm."

Chapter Five:
Shadow People?

Travel writer Logan Hawkes talks of having encountered shadowy entities in the Big Bend National Park. He describes how, a few years ago as he was travelling through it with a friend, they stopped at the hot springs to relax in the water for a while and enjoy the peaceful beauty of the area as it grew to darkness around them.

Finally it became pitch dark and they stared up at the sky counting the stars. Suddenly they could see what looked like silhouetted shadows of a group of people, standing on a ledge away up the river. He and his friend expected the group might approach them and became a little anxious. They waited with trepidation, knowing no-one else was around for miles.

Finally, after not seeing them move and hearing no sounds of talking coming from them, they shone the flashlight over at them to see them more clearly.

"Except there were no figures in the light, then turning the light off the faint silhouette outlines re-appeared."

Unnerved after repeating the exercise a couple more times and seeing the same response, they didn't hang around and quickly climbed out of the water, keen to get their clothes back on and get out of there.

"To this day we cannot say who or what they were. But I can confidently tell you they were not living beings."

Texas isn't the only State where these elusive and hard to define 'shadow beings' have been seen. In the Santa Lucia Mountains along the central coast of California, it was known that the Native Americans told of 'Dark Watchers'; shadowed figures who would appear on ledges as dusk fell into night. Human-like ghost figures, always dark shadows, standing silhouetted against the landscape.

Who they are, and what they want no-one knows, but many have seen them. Usually it seems they disappear without coming any closer. Many have speculated about them, and others have told of their encounter in forums on the internet.

'Weird California,' has a collection of compelling and highly mysterious contributions from witnesses who have written in to tell of their sightings;

L Brennan of Ramona, wrote: "While flying my aircraft I glanced toward the Range and saw what looked to be seven very large dark figures standing there."

"We saw a very large dark figure," says another, "standing at the edge of the mountain, staring off into the distance; it was over 10 ft tall. It seemed to have a cape, with broad shoulders... extremely weird; I travel that road daily. This was around September 2010."

In a slightly different account, G Garner says, "We see them here; they're almost like horses on their hind legs in the dusk."

***

Then, just as mysteriously, a lady from Tennessee recently called the Mutual UFO Network, not knowing who else to call and needing to urgently talk about what had just happened to her that morning.

It was around 6am and she was standing on the deck of her house drinking an early morning coffee, enjoying the warm and quiet beginning to her day, when suddenly she saw something that defied explanation.

The deck of her house was at an elevation of twelve feet from the ground below. When she turned around to go back into the house, she stopped dead. She could not fail to see the huge black shadow; the shape of a man but standing higher than the deck.

It was leaning against it. It was the shape of a man yet it appeared to have no face. She was frozen to the spot, unable to move.

Suddenly it turned its 'head' toward her. Then she watched as very slowly it peeled itself off the rail. It ran its fingers slowly along the side of the rail as though it was coming in her direction. Then it started floating away.

It had legs but it wasn't touching the ground as it walked. It moved its legs like a man would.

Then as it got some distance away, it turned back around in her direction again. She felt very sure that it was communicating the message to her that though it had left her unharmed; it was more than capable of hurting her if it chose to do so...

In Missouri too there's been sightings in a place that's called 'Zombie Road,' near the Mahoning River not too far from Ohio. A photo exists of what appears to show a group of Shadow People, standing along a tree line above a small lake.

It was taken in March 2005 by paranormal investigator Tom Halstead prior to his death. There are no reflections of their bodies in the water below.

It seems from accounts of those who have reportedly seen them, that 'The Watchers' are less sinister than the 'Shadow people.' While the Watchers do not seem to interfere with humans, unless those who have encountered them up close are no longer around to speak for what happened, it would seem that they prefer to be left alone. Shadow people however, according to medium Toiny Braden, "Are evil and full of malicious intent; those are the ones you never want to see. I've felt such intense levels of malice," she says, of the ones she's seen around her when assisting clients they've been terrorising.

***

In Kent, England, 1963, four young men said they saw a bright light descend from the sky as they took a walk through the woods one night. The glowing light then proceeded to follow them, stalking behind them, much to their confusion and horror.

One of the boys, John Flaxton, said the orb, hovering at a height just taller than them followed stealthily behind them. After some time, it moved behind some trees and they hoped it was leaving them, but instead as they watched, a horrifying black 'apparition' appeared, a jet black figure the height of a man but with no face. It looked as *though* it had wings, but they fled as fast as they could in sheer terror before it could get them.

One of his companions, Mervyn later described it as having webbed feet but no head.

The local Reverend, told the Press,

"Several youths have told me of strange things they've seen. All of them were very frightened and they've definitely seen 'something.'

***

Located northeast of Colorado Springs lies The Black Forest; a heavily wooded area amidst which is a home on a five acre plot that in the late 1990's had everyone, from the local Sheriffs, to Hopi shaman and even a

Congressman believing that something sinisterly supernatural was there.

Steve and Beth Lee moved in to the home with their two sons. Strange things soon started happening. Numerous dark shadows and orbs of light would appear. There was often a strange chemical smell, and each of the family members would suffer regularly from burning eyes and throats.

In an effort to try to understand what was going on, thinking it must be people doing it, Mr Lee installed a high-tech security system to try to capture them. As soon as he'd installed it, the motion sensors would go off many times during the day and night, causing the alarms to ring out; and yet each time they could find no persons on their property.

Police responding to their numerous calls could find no sign of any intruders.

The children talked of seeing 'Shadow people.'

Startlingly, when the Lees replayed their security films they would see unexplained floating orbs, outlines of human forms, and even images of faces.

A local Hopi shaman came, and on investigation claimed that the property was located on a vortex that opened up to another dimension, allowing beings from that dimension to enter ours. Psychic detectives and paranormal investigators arrived to carry out their own investigations, all of whom appeared to capture the same troubling images, including translucent faces and dark human-like forms.

It seemed that no matter what different photographic tools were used; the images always appeared, ruling out any kind of trickery or malfunction of equipment.

In a bizarre twist to the story however, Mr Lee claimed that the phenomenon captured at his forest home was in fact not paranormal, but was the culmination of him being targeted by "Agencies of the US government," harassing him using electromagnetic technologies.

Mr Lees felt this was because, in his belief, their home was close to a government facility where 'mind control,' and other such experiments were being secretly carried out, heavily guarded from the outside by a military presence.

It wasn't only Shadow people that he was claiming to see.

"Outside I saw men in snow-camouflage. I got my rifle and started walking toward them."

They shouted a warning to him.

"I got within a few feet of them and they disappeared; just vanished. There were no tracks."

Another time, something even more bizarre occurred. Accompanied by friends, they all watched through infra-red binoculars as a team of men disappeared into a neighbour's doghouse!

He claimed there were at least a dozen of them, and putting down their binoculars they ran toward the men shouting out at them, yet the men appeared not to hear them.

He speculated afterward, "Did we actually see it or was it a hologram? If someone had told me this I would have said they're nuts, but the best thing to do in a War is to make them (the enemy) see things; after that they wouldn't put up a fight."

He feels that the images of soldiers, ghosts, and the shadow people his family and friends have seen are all being created by some kind of technological experimentation.

He hears disembodied voices threatening to kill him and his children. In his house; in his car.

"This isn't supernatural; someone is spending a lot of time and money trying to make it look like it is."

Mystery dizziness, nausea and fever have repeatedly hit them and those living nearby too. He claims hospital tests could find no answers.

Was he experiencing some kind of paranoid breakdown, was a demon trying to control him, or was it really even more sinister, as he suggests?

Another person, a man called Russell Elliot has also come forward to state that he's experienced strange events near his own home in the Black Forest, only a few minutes away from the Lees house. Mr Elliot too began capturing recordings of odd incidents, including strange lights around his home, to the extent of even posting YouTube videos of what he claims to be an alien being. His claims are as yet unsubstantiated.

Perhaps there really is something going on at the Lees property however. Mind Control through Holographic projections? Voice to skull microwaves making him hear voices?

Psychotronic weapons being developed to invisibly lock onto a victim and attack them subliminally? Bio-electromagnetic weapons; sending lasers, beams, or sound waves that work in stealth at the speed of light; able to disarm, attack, and even capable of killing a person? Directed energy weapons?

Do they all really exist? Can they interfere with a person's state of mind; sending threats or self-destructive thoughts, or even causing much worse?

***

Others say the Archons are behind many of these types of manifestations of voices and apparitions.

'Deceivers,' who can mimic and take on forms in response to human belief systems.

Our interactions with shadow figures, spirits, extraterrestrials, ancient aliens, Djinn, humanoids and crypto's, are all said to involve these mysterious Archons.

The theory goes that Reptilians, Bigfoot, and all 'Paranormal' entities, are merely avatars that are manifested in the 'matrix' by a control system.

The suggestion is that whether alien, demonic, or Fey, they are all different forms of manifestation brought into being by a control system; a universal intelligence in control of us all.

Who; or what that 'pattern maker' is, and for what purpose it is operating the control system, no-one seems to be able to define or prove.

The belief is however, that it's malign and malevolent, and intent on creating fear and causing terror and destruction.

From the evidence of reported sightings and encounters, that would appear to be the case.

Ancient Gnostic texts say the Archons are inorganic beings that emerged in the world before Earth was formed and before humans came into creation. They envy the human form because they cannot take that form, and with this envy they come into our realm intent on causing havoc and harm, seeking to hurt us. They inhabit their own realm but manage to temporarily enter ours, taking these disparate forms to interfere with us.

This thesis is a 'catch all;' it implies that every strange sighting or 'paranormal' encounter exists only as some kind of holographic form, and that they are all one and the same in origin.

It's hard to imagine anyone who has encountered one of these many different and very sinister entities as saying that they are the same 'indefinable' thing however. Witnesses would most certainly say that they were all too frighteningly real.

The ancient Mystery School of thought is that these intruders are strong enough to negatively influence us, have the ability to affect and play with our minds; they can disturb our sanity through devious means such as telepathy and suggestion.

As well as appearing in physical form as grotesque and frightening figures, in the form of Fairies, Demons, Aliens, or disfigured and partly formed monsters, it's also thought they can attack invisibly to disorient us, confuse us, mislead and misdirect us. They can even send self-destructive notions into our minds. Telling a person to do something that will lead to injury and even fatality. Telling a person they want to cause injury or death to themselves.

Are they behind the demise or disappearance of so many?

Chapter Six:
Spirit Helpers?

While it's believed 'spirits' or shadow people are usually malevolent, there are also accounts of mysterious 'spirit beings' helping stranded travellers.

On 1st June 1933, Frank Smythe was alone on Mount Everest. One by one, the rest of his team had turned back, too exhausted to continue, and the Expedition was left with just him to try to conquer the world's highest peak. He was up an altitude of over 26,000 ft; where the level of oxygen in the air is almost insufficient to keep a human being alive.

Smythe described being absolutely overwhelmed with exhaustion and a desperate hopelessness. He had only 1,000 feet left to the top, yet he was so weak. Standing for a few moments, he said, "on the very boundaries of life and death," he reached for a piece of cake in his pocket, to try to give him the last tiny ounce of strength he needed.

"I turned round with one half in my hand to offer it to my companion."

But he was completely alone. During that last desperate struggle against the elements, he had thought that he was being accompanied by someone. Though initially too embarrassed to talk openly about the experience for fear of ridicule, he did document it in his official reports.

He wrote: 'All the time that I was alone, I had a feeling that I was being accompanied. The feeling was so strong.'

Psychologist Peter Suedfeld and writer John Geiger, term this quite common experience in remote and risky environments 'a sensed presence experience'; a kind of subconscious coping mechanism in extreme environments.

They say the 'presences' themselves can vary in their appearance, identity, and their behaviour. They can include what appear to be angelic visitations, ghosts, or 'someone' seen or heard.

***

In Newsweek Magazine, December, 1993, a tragic story was covered about a young woman Chantel Lakey, and her fiancé Dale, who wanted to show her the view from a trail as they travelled along the Pacific highway 101. It was an area of dense forest with steep cliffs overhanging the coast.

They managed to climb to the top of the trail quite easily, but it was as they started to descend that they ran into trouble. Dale had seen an animal trail and thought it would be possible to descend it, however as they headed down they soon realised they had taken a very precarious path, as it virtually turned into a cliff of loose shale and rock.

It began to rain and the path became even more treacherous. It wasn't possible now to head back up and they had no option but to continue. Dale walked in front, turning around every few steps to help Chantel. As he turned around again, his foot slipped and without warning he fell to his death.

Chantel froze in shock and terror. Clutching onto the loose rock, she was unable to move.

She says "I had no particular faith in the being that others call God, but I think desperation draws out of us deep feelings we never knew we had."

She cried out to God, and describes that all of a sudden "it was as though the gateway between Heaven and Earth had opened up, and I saw Angels all around me, like a wall of protection, holding me, closing in around me."

She clung on and yet the next thing she remembers is looking up and seeing the cliff above her. "Somehow I'd managed to descend."

When the rescue team later went to retrieve her fiancé's body, they could not go down the cliff path that Chantel had descended, declaring the route impossible even with their experience and equipment.

* * *

Bill Burt, who's been a national reporter in the UK for decades, is someone for whom angel stories have figured heavily but purely incidentally in some of the News events he's gone to cover.

Mr Burt describes one odd incident when he went to cover a story about two schoolboys missing on a climbing trip in the mountains in Scotland. By the time he arrived the schoolboys had fortunately already been found; however, when he interviewed them they told him of how a woman in a white dress had approached them high up on the mountain and beckoned them to follow her. The lost boys didn't stop to think about it, they simply followed her and she led them straight toward the search party that was out looking for them.

When Burt later spoke to the leader of the search party, repeating the story the boys had told him, the leader stated that neither him nor anyone else in the search party had seen a woman with the boys.

Chapter Seven:
Mysterious Cases of Children Going Missing

A short news item in the July 2nd 1964 issue of the New York Times reported on the strange case of a three year old girl.

'A search party of 400 men found today a 3 year-old girl who'd been missing from her home for 17 hours. She was dishevelled, but otherwise in good condition.'

The child, Monica Mei, daughter of Armando Mei a well-known New York restaurant owner, had wandered away at some point from the family's summer home on Paradise Island in Orange County. Ernest Wippenger, a Middletown school crossing guard, had found the child huddled among rocks on top of Paradise Mountain, at an elevation of 1,606 feet.

Douglas Kinnear, Orange County Fire Coordinator, said the child had presumably walked across a footbridge connecting the 14 acre Nevesink River Island to the mainland, and then scaled the mountain.

The party of volunteers searching the thickly wooded area had included Police, Firemen and bloodhounds to try to pick up her scent. They had searched through the night and had already passed through the area where she was eventually found alive.

The 1,606 ft Mt Paradise is located in the most remote section of the A.T. in New Jersey. It has to be asked how the child managed to climb the mountain, and why she had done so, as well as why the trackers were unable to find her scent from the area she went missing?

A similar but much more tragic incident occurred back in the winter of 1890, when Ottie Powell was four years old. He was at school in rural Amherst County, Virginia, when his school mistress asked the children to go out to the woods around the school house to collect some timber for the classroom stove.

As all the children returned back indoors it was soon realised that Ottie was not among them. Immediately the school mistress sent the other children to their homes nearby to collect their parents and begin a search for the missing boy. The school was within the George Washington National Forest, on the Appalachian Trail, by Bluff Mountain, and surrounded by thick woodland.

Hundreds of neighbours and friends began a desperate search, spreading out in circles from the school, but they could find no trace of Ottie. Snow started falling heavily and an ice storm started, and it became impossible to continue searching the mountain for him. By evening, they had to stop.

Over the next few days and weeks, hundreds of volunteers continued searching the area, but to no avail.

Seven months later, on April 3, 1892, seven miles away on the top of the mountain, hunters heard their dog barking, and followed its trail up a steep path that led to the top of the mountain. There they found the remains of the little boy.

Everyone in the area, and those reading the newspaper accounts nationally, were baffled as to how and why the young boy had managed to climb his way over rocks, through hedges, and up cliffs to this lofty peak at the altitude of 3,350 feet, barefoot.

Local garden blogger Jeanne Grunert wrote recently of her hike up the mountain, commenting that it felt like walking up flights of stairs for two hours without stopping. On reaching the top she noticed the memorial there to the child. She says, 'his body was found on this spot – How had a four year old child wandered up a mountain that we had found so difficult to climb?'

* * *

The May 27, 1922 edition of the New York Times covered the bizarre story of a young girl in a small Brittany village who went missing.

"A baffling mystery is exciting the inhabitants of the small Brittany village of Goas Al Ludu, in the Brest district, (France). Early in April a little girl, Pauline Picard, disappeared from her parent's farm, all searches proving fruitless. However, as her parents had virtually given up all hope of ever finding their daughter, it was reported from the far away town of Cherbourg, that a small girl had been found there, whose age and appearance corresponded very similarly to that of the missing Pauline.

Her parents hurried to Cherbourg and said with much relief that the child was theirs. Strangely, however, it was reported that the child did not seem to recognise her parents and remained mute when addressed in the Breton dialect she had grown up speaking.

Taken home, the child was recognised by neighbours, and as such the terrible incident was concluded as reaching a happy ending.

However, the newspaper continues the story, 'Yesterday a startling discovery was made which makes the whole affair more mysterious than ever.'

A farmer crossing a field about a mile away discovered the horribly mutilated body of a small girl, entirely naked and decapitated. Close by, carefully folded, lay her clothes. The farmer returned with the Police and several villagers, including the Picard's, who instantly recognised the clothes as those worn by Pauline the day she disappeared. The body could not be identified. If the body was that of Pauline, who was the child the parents were already claiming was Pauline?

So thorough was the search carried out at the time of the little girl's disappearance, says the newspaper, that the body would have been discovered had it been lying all along where it was found. 'Everything now points to the theory that it was placed there, together with the neatly folded clothes,' it states.

The prolific Fortean writer of the time, Charles Fort wrote about the case too. 'It could not long have been lying, so conspicuous, but unseen. The body placed in a conspicuous position, as if planning to have it found? It seems that the clothes, also conspicuous, had not been lying there for several weeks, subject to the disturbing effects of rains and wind. They were "neatly folded."

***

The UK Spectator Magazine issue of May 3rd 1902, detailed what they called 'a strange story,' regarding a young boy William Llewellyn, 'who three weeks ago unaccountably disappeared in the street of a Welsh town, and whose body was discovered on the summit of a Glamorganshire hill on Saturday last.'

It is reported that the boy disappeared from a shop he was in with his mother.

'Every possible effort was made to find him, but it was not until more than a fortnight had passed that his dead body was found,' unintentionally by fox hounds.

The coroner said there was no evidence of a crime.

The magazine asks, trying to understand the unusual circumstances, 'Is there any plausible theory?'

It writes; 'Here are the facts. All hills, roads, fields were thoroughly examined. The child's boots are stated not to have been dirty. The child was five; the spot where he

52

was found is some 1,850 feet. His boots were *not dirty*. His body was found ten miles away from where he was last seen. If he walked at all, he probably walked more miles. Could a child of that age do that?'

'Is it not remarkable that the body was found on the summit of the highest, most inaccessible hill in the area? Why? The instinct of a person lost is to go down, not up. He knows that the homes are in the valleys, not on summits. It is one of the strangest things that has come to light for some years.'

'Do we solve it by saying it was just an instance of 'superhuman' endurance, and total failure in a power of reasoning?' they ask.

His coat was placed beside him. He had no injuries apart from abrasions to his hands. It was ruled that he had been dead for a number of days, but not as long as the amount of time he had been missing for.

The newspaper also makes mention of the possibility that someone took him there to the highest spot, placing him there to die. It's interesting perhaps to recollect the Inca's tradition of ritual sacrifices on the summits of mountains. The mummified bodies of three children were found on the top of the Volcan Llullaillaco Mountain in the Andes, in 1999.

It was found upon DNA analysis of their preserved hair, that they were heavily drugged with maze alcohol and cocoa in the months prior to their sacrifice; it's presumed in order to make them more compliant and calm when it came to the time for them to be sacrificed.

Dr Andrew Wilson at the University of Bedfordshire, who carried out the analysis, calls it 'chilling.'

In the area where the mummies were found, there are thought to exist up to fifty sacrifice sites alone.

* * *

In October 1917, a young boy from Hampden went missing from his backyard near a place dubbed, 'The Forest of the Dead.'

Native Americans believed it was a cursed place of evil spirits, and it seems that the area has gained an unsettling reputation for mysterious disappearances.

Horror writer Joseph Rubas spent some time researching the history of this area of the Berkshire Mountains, in New England.

According to Rubas, when the boy disappeared the local Army Commander volunteered three hundred of his men to search for him. They found no tracks of where the boy had gone; no sign of him.

Eventually, a sheriff's deputy discovered the young boy, miles from his home asleep in a thicket.

The writer claims that from his research, during the search several of the soldiers searching for the boy themselves disappeared in the mountain, never to be seen again. The strange incident raises questions not only of how the young boy had traveller so far on his own, but also of the soldiers' inexplicable disappearances.

***

In the Pennsylvanian Allegheny Mountains two young boys went missing back in 1856. Nearly two hundred people rapidly began searching for them through the dense hill tops and ravines. They could find no trace of the boys, but for ten days they wouldn't give up. Everyone got involved, closing their businesses and stopping work to help in the search, knowing the unforgiving wildness of the area they were lost in.

Many stayed out at night, lighting fires on various spots across the mountain, hoping to draw the children toward one of them. While many searchers took a new route on the mountain each day, others would travel back over the ground they had already covered, guessing that the children could have come back to that part of the mountain in their wandering.

As the days went by without a trace of them, speculation and rumour began amongst the community; they were killed by a wild beast, they'd been kidnapped, their parents had murdered them.

Then, a farmer named Jacob Dibert who lived a few miles away began to have recurring nightmares. Several nights in a row, he dreamt that he was with the search party when he became separated from them, and discovered the boys.

Unfamiliar with the forest area himself, though he thought himself crazy, he described to his wife the detailed scene in his dreams and asked her if she knew of an area like it in the mountains. She replied that there was such an area.

Upon telling his brother-in-law about the dream too, his brother-in-law thought it impossible; for the boys to have got to the location in Jacob's dreams, they would have to have gone approximately six miles from their home and crossed a wide fast running creek, and climbed high. The two boys, George and Joseph Cox were only aged five and seven; he thought it impossible.

However, perplexed by such unaccustomed and disturbing nightmares, Jacob felt he had to investigate, and so his brother-in-law led him to the area he described. They reached a hollow, saw a deer he had described dead just like in his dreams, crossed over the creek and hiked up a steep ravine on the opposite side, where they saw the shoe of one of the boys he had also described from his nightmares. Shortly after, they found the boys bodies in the exact position he had described.

Spookily accurate, his nightmares had told him where to find the children, though tragically they had died of exposure by then.

Several aspects of this case are disturbing; not only the fact that the man seemingly had cognitive dreams telling him how to find them, but also that the boys had ended up where they did.

What on earth had made them cross a creek and climb upwards into the mountains, knowing they were going far from home?

Chapter Eight:
Snatched by Something Under the Ground?

Ufologist Scott Corrales refers to the densely forested National Forest in Puerto Rico as somewhere "that has a dark side which involves human disappearances."

A huge number of people have vanished from El Yunque forest, without any explanation for their disappearances. Park authorities tend to explain that they are caused simply by natural geography, such as sinkholes and yet, as the investigator points out, many of the disappearances have happened in parts of the forests where these natural landscapes features are not part of the terrain, and are indeed far from the site of the existence of these dangerous sinkholes or the possibility of quicksand.

He quotes as an example a report by native investigator Hermes Rivera, who published details of an incident in the late 1970's which told the tragic story of a group of children who had all disappeared inside the forest on a school trip there. The police even turned to a psychic, whose statement about their fate was chilling. He said they were no longer in this physical dimension.

The children were never found. The teacher in charge of the group, unable to cope with the sadness and feeling responsible for them, ended up killing himself because they had never been found.

Even armed soldiers, he discovered, have seemingly disappeared. In March 1976, two Marines stationed at a nearby naval base vanished inside the national park.

The area itself is rife with speculation as many locals report seeing strange lights coming from the mountain of El Yunque; reports of UFO sightings, alien craft and even sightings of humanoid beings suddenly appearing on the trails in front of hikers. Others say there is unusual military activity going on in the area.

American Navy Officer Jorge Martin, in the journal UFO Evidence reports that in 1993 during a trip to the mountain, without being aware of it, two visitors, N. Berríos and J.Ruiz, took a number of photographs that when looked at later, appeared to show a humanoid-like being standing near a rock close by.

When questioned about what he believed it was, J. Ruiz said in his opinion, "That's not from here; and people have for so long been saying that strange things are happening; I'd say that *they're* here; we're not alone. That is a fact."

The editor relates another case involving multiple witnesses. 'It was in February 1991, about 3am, just next to the Forestry Service hut. Police Officer Torres had been with his wife and a group of friends when in astonishment they saw close-by, two extraordinarily odd 'beings' walking down the road.

Jose Martin makes the statement that there are bases inside the mountains in which he and many other navy personnel have seen UFO's enter somehow, through the mountain itself. He told researcher Timothy Good of his claim that a large secret subterranean alien base was there, going deep under the sea, and built by an alien race.

"It is a base that appears to be extraterrestrial. We have been watching the situation for years - and we know that they are down there," he says.

***

'Alien-hunters,' like John Rhodes, believe there are many of these underground bases hidden in Mountains in the States and in other countries including England, and that a greatly advanced race who come from the 'Draco Star System,' want to take over the human race; Others say they already have, with mind control.

There have been thousands of reports over the years of ordinary people claiming to have been abducted by Reptilian beings, and 'abduction investigator' John Carpenter states he has worked with over one hundred 'victims.'

He says these entities are reported as looking virtually the same by everyone he talks to; as standing at least seven feet tall, with lizard scales all over their bodies. Their faces, he says, are described as a cross between that of a human and a snake. Their eyes are almond shaped, with vertical slits, and their mouths have no lips."

They are said to be highly evolved super-intelligent creatures, extremely strong, with muscular bodies and powerful arms. Perhaps most disturbingly it's said that they can shape-shift and impose holograms onto their faces to give them a human appearance. Contactees have said that they drain the victim of all energy so that they are helpless to resist.

***

In the 1940's, a peculiar story emerged. A man called Richard Shaver began to tell an extraordinary if not completely outlandish tale, starting with how during his job at a factory, he began to hear other people's thoughts. As if that wasn't enough, what he said next was mind-blowing.

He claimed that the "voices" he heard were coming from below the ground, where warring alien species were battling each other. These entities he called 'The Dero' and 'The Tero' races; which he claimed, with their advanced technology were capable of transmitting electronically-enhanced telepathic brain waves.

He said he'd been taken to the underground place, led there by a holographic image of a being, through a hidden entrance. The 'Teros' were friendly, but he said the enemy 'Deros' were planting thoughts in his head to make him sound ridiculous, so that no-one would believe what he said about the existence of these underground bases and to prevent the public from taking him seriously, because they feared their bases were soon going to become public knowledge.

According to Shaver, the 'Deros' kidnapped people from above ground by the hundreds and took them below, to use them for meat.

He said this species were capable of causing accidents, disasters and illnesses to people, and that they already exerted incredible power over the unsuspecting general public, who did not know they were being systematically mind-controlled remotely.

The editor of the magazine Amazing Stories, who covered his story, claimed that while in the presence of Shaver he heard several different voices emanate from Shaver as he talked aloud, and that chillingly, the voices were discussing the murder of a woman in one of the underground bases.

It all sounded like a mix of paranoia and a bad science fiction plot, and of course many declared him a loony; however, hundreds of subsequently people wrote in to the magazine in response to the details Shaver gave, claiming that they too had had experiences with an underground world. Were they all insane?

***

In the early '60's, the story of Thomas Castello came out. He alleged that he worked as a security officer at a top secret underground facility in New Mexico. His job was to ensure the security of surveillance equipment there; but he soon found himself taking secret photos of the base, appalled at the activities going on there.

Located several miles underground, experiments were being carried out on human abductees by lizard-like reptilian creatures, he said, who controlled their victims using telepathy and mind manipulation techniques.

Castello said he had seen horrifying genetic monsters in the Laboratories, and that any humans who did not survive the experiments were fed to these Reptilians.

He also claimed that the Native Americans in the area understood that the base existed and spoke of the "underground 'life-forms', such as Bigfoot, that were spotted outside near the base.

Fearing for his life, he went on the run and disappeared; meanwhile his family he left behind, also mysteriously 'disappeared.'

***

Another character, a man by the name of Billie Woodard, once in the US Air Force, claimed that as a young boy he was abducted while walking home one day and taken through a vortex opening down into the earth.

The beings down there used Vortexes that they created, to act as exit points from their Hollow Earth bases, he said, enabling themselves and creatures such as the Sasquatch to come through.

He's been speaking out about his experiences for years, and claims that though the Government try to silence him, he is 'protected,' and impossible to harm. Many proponents believe his thesis and stories.

***

Writer K. Kizziar claims to have been abducted by Reptilians inhabiting an underground base in the Superstition Mountains of Arizona.

According to Kizziar, these beings dressed in dark robes use humans as their slaves inside the base as well as above ground; mind controlled to do their bidding. They kidnap their victims and take them below to their bases.

While these stories sound impossible to believe, it's interesting to note that many interested in the phenomenon of disappearing people have identified similarities between the alleged existence of maps showing the location of these underground bases and areas where there have also been a high proportion of people vanishing too.

**

Another outlandish story of activities underground comes this time from researcher Radu Cinamar, who broke the news of a startling discovery in the Bucegi Mountains of Romania.

The Bucegi Mountains are reported to be extremely mysterious. Some have been prompted by a number of cases of missing persons to claim that the area of the stunningly beautiful Carpathians have an altogether other-worldly character to them.

People mysteriously disappear, either never to re-appear again or appear in some other place, unable to tell what happened to them. Elders there tell of people disappearing in 'fogs' or being 'thrown' into other places from where they were hiking, done so by an 'invisible force.'

Other hikers tell of a euphoric feeling that comes over them, of an almost hypnotised sensation, of not feeling any tiredness or exertion on climbing the Mountain, reminiscent of some of the accounts from Zimbabwe's Inyangani Mountain. Electronic devices often stop working.

Geologist Dimitri Stanica says he has felt 'something special' in the area in terms of its geo-magnetic energy properties, and indeed there are stories of miracle healings occurring there. Once a year a magical 'shadow pyramid' appears around a Sphinx shaped stone at the summit.

In 2003, it was claimed by the researcher Cinamar that US military satellites had discovered two artificial energy blocks in the Mountains. The satellites seemed to show the first one was blocking access to a tunnel, while the second was a dome shape inside the middle of the mountain.

It was said to closely match a similar energy structure discovered in Iraq and which conspirators such as academic researcher Dr Michael Salla claim was the real reason for the Iraq War; in order to enable the US to enter this structure and seize the discoveries of advanced technology inside.

The 'find' was initially reported on Antenna 1, the local television channel; after which on YouTube is a snippet of the news presenter receiving an anonymous telephone death threat and being told to maintain silence over the subject.

Opponents have claimed Antenna 1 is a sensationalist TV channel not to be taken seriously.

There were claims of the US & Romanian Governments rushing to quash the information, and interference from the Illuminati, all determined not to enable the controversial and highly secretive contents from being discovered by the world. It would change our current belief systems and they did not want that to happen.

Cinamar and Peter Moon wrote of the discovery and what was found inside the mountain; three US Special Forces military, on touching the energy barrier were reported to have died instantly, but using technology they somehow broke through the barrier.

Inside, through a tunnel that appeared mined, they came to a huge gallery that seemed of a synthetic nature yet was the colour of oil. Green and blue lights glowed, reflecting the energy shields inside.

It was here that they allegedly found a holographic Hall of Records, left there by an advanced civilization and detailing the 'true' origins of man and civilisation, along with the most advanced technology ever found, including capability for time travel, and far beyond the current known physics concepts.

It was claimed that a race of Giants had left these secrets; their skeletons left behind as evidence.

There were also three mysterious tunnels leading into the Inner Earth.

If true, this would seem not the only anomaly of the mountain range. A Romanian Professor, Constantine Badger, also claimed to have entered a tunnel in the mountains of Ceahlau, also in Romania, and discovered underground chambers there, several miles deep.

He claims that he was contacted by an 'intelligence' that led him to the tunnels and inside was enabled to jump space and time, going through the tunnels at a speed ordinarily unachievable by foot.

The editor of *FaraSecrete* Romanian journal also relates a strange occurrence that allegedly happened prior to the underground Buecgi discoveries. In 1980, two siblings who were both highly experienced climbers were scaling the mountain. A quarter of a way from the summit, something caught the eye of one of them. He observed unusual archaic lettering carved in the stone of a narrow ledge. Beside it was a gold coloured item that appeared to be a chain. As the man went toward it and touched it, he apparently vanished.

His brother climbed up to the ledge and could see no sign of his brother there. At first the police refused to believe his account, yet he showed several witnesses the object that looked to be embedded in the stone.

The editor claims that after that incident, the area was permanently closed for access and Government investigators began to study the unusual rock-face and its alleged powers.

Interestingly, long before the Bucegi tunnels discovery, Professor Ernst Muldashev wrote of the discovery of caves on Mount Kailash in Tibet where soldiers attempting to enter them were overpowered by a strange and powerful force that caused them extreme nausea and severe head pain, some even having heart attacks and dying.

Are there geometric anomolies which can cause the disappearance of people, or is there something ancient and far more powerful underneath the ground?

Is time travel technology somehow involved?

***

Olav Phillips is founder of the *Anomalies Network*, a database resource which he claims has more than 140,000 reported sightings of paranormal anomalies, including of the UFO type.

In a recent article, he wrote of his opinion in regard to the mysterious disappearances of people in remote forest and mountain regions, referring to them as possibly being part of 'Batch Consignments,' taken as slaves to other planets.

A fairly large workforce would be needed, he reasoned, the work would be tough, and the death rate high due to the danger of the work and the hostile environment. So, you would need a constant supply of new people being kidnapped to provide the labour force.

'Where do you get large numbers of people over a long term?' he asks. 'Every year hundreds of people go missing under mysterious circumstances. There are disappearances which actually defy conventional logic.'

His implication is that the people who do disappear mysteriously without trace in the forests and mountains are being taken.

While it is a possibility, and while some think the number of people disappearing in wilderness areas is far higher than has been recorded, one does have to disagree that the number is anywhere near high enough to provide a significant workforce, and while young children go missing in forests, so too do the elderly, and these would not be of great use as a hard-labour workforce.

Many more people go missing in urban areas though, and as he points out, in war-torn and highly unstable regions hundreds if not thousands will simply disappear, so perhaps it could be said that the reality of these examples do lend credence to the 'batch consignments' theory being a distinct possibility.

One perhaps surprising proponent of the belief in a base on Mars comes in the form of Laura Eisenhower, the great-granddaughter of former US President Dwight Eisenhower. Not long ago she went public with an extraordinary claim.

Speaking on many radio shows, Laura Eisenhower claimed she had been lured into a pact to Teleport to Mars by her then lover, who she later believed had deliberately targeted her. Eisenhower described that after meeting the man who she formed a relationship with he gradually told her that he was attached to a secret Mars colony project.

The reason for the secret Mars colony he told her, was apparently to provide a survival civilization for the human race, should the earth be destroyed by something such as HAARP, a giant magnetic pulse strike, or nuclear or bio weapons.

A situation which really occurred? It is indeed possible, although perhaps not so convincing is her further statement; 'For the Mars colony to have control, they wanted the Magdalene (blood).' She goes on to say that through the many psychic readings she has had, it has been confirmed to her that she has this bloodline.

While being abducted to be taken to other planets may or may not be happening, there are some compelling testimonies available on the web from those who believe the batch consignment theory applies to bases underground, below the rural wilderness areas.

Chapter Nine:
Military Involvement in
Disappearances?

Mary Joyce is an avid researcher of underground bases and their alien connection, with particular interest in trying to discover new activity and current construction going on related to military involvement. Joyce says she's heard many witness reports about secret military activity, particularly in the Smoky Mountains National Park.

In early 2013, what she calls 'a credible ex-military witness' spoke with her about the activity. He spoke of sightings of 'Rangers' carrying machine guns, he spoke of loud boom sounds in the area. He said there were many others who've seen unusual things in the Park, including actual employees of the Park but claimed that they are afraid to talk about those things.

She spoke to a lady called Jane Spottedbird about her trip in 2013 to a landmark off the Blue Ridge Parkway in North Carolina. When she discovered the road leading to it was closed, she left her car and decided to walk up. What struck her as she walked along was that she couldn't hear the sounds of any birds nearby. It was eerily quiet.

What she did begin to hear however, were deep and resonating booms. "They reminded me of the type of equipment that's used to pound pylons into the ground. I went to the overhang to look and see where some construction was maybe going on. The boom sound continued all the time I was there, and at one point was continuous. By then, it was hard for me to think clearly. Since then, I've discovered that others who've got too close to a secret facility have been caused the same distress. Perhaps some kind of electro-magnetic 'pulse' is being used?" she speculates.

***

Controversial scholar Alex Putney makes the claim that those who point the finger of blame at Bigfoot or other entities for causing the mysterious disappearances of people in forests and woodlands, are doing so as disinformation artists on behalf of the CIA; to divert attention from and to cover up these CIA/military led abductions, to prevent people from discovering the existence of military-industrial installations secretly running below the ground, full of people.

He goes further; "The existence of dozens of these secret underground military bases were clearly exposed, he says, by surviving Nazi commander Otto Skorzeny, lifelong comrade of Hitler. One such base was identified as a breeding ground for the Nazi elite below Glacier National Park."

Researcher and futurist Michael Lindemann has spoken of what he calls the new 'Noah's Ark,' underground, to describe what he believes the US government has in effect been building. 'Underground bases, all over the world; huge bases that would shock you; able to support tens of thousands; to 'save' an elite, the 'cream,' who will survive the apocalypse.'

A Dr Steven Greer claims he has collected up to two hundred top-secret military, intelligence and corporate witness testimonies to secret projects that detail a covert alien/government agenda.

Researcher Miles Johnston of *The Bases Project* has filmed hours of testimony from a man named Barry King, who claims to have been a security member at one of the secret underground Bases in England, where he says the purpose is Mind Control and other experimentation on human abductees. He claims there are bases at Peasemore, Berkshire, and Greenham Common, also Berkshire, approximately fifty miles from London.

He states that abducted children and adults were used for both mind control and genetic testing. The 'aliens' were not doing this he says; the people running the bases *created* these aliens and programmed them. They are generated life-forms he says. These aliens were then used to abduct people, he alleges.

King first started making these claims in the '90's and still to this day maintains it is not fantasy. However more commonly now he claims that it's not the aliens who are doing the abductions but rather 'MILAB's;' human 'black ops' snatching people and convincing them they have been abducted by aliens with the use of generated and holographic images.

Recently in the most outlandish turn of events, self-titled British 'Super Soldiers' going by the names of James Casbolt and Max Speirs have claimed that they were both taken into bases as children and held there for years while they were 'programmed' by mind control techniques. They claim it was not Alien-led, but instead led by terrestrial 'black ops' projects and done with explicit complicity of the Military, Government, and elite Secret Societies, both in the US and UK. Indeed their claims go very deep in terms of who was really involved.

Occult ritual is used and much of it involves the harnessing of ancient demonic power by the 'power elite' according to 'whistleblower' Casbolt.

Some of his claims include that through the use of advanced alien technology, these trained abductees are able to 'remote view' victims. Occult symbolism is used for added power. Called 'Project Mannequin' he claimed he and other child abductees were 'weaponized' to remotely cause heart attacks or death to 'targets.'

Their stories make for fascinating listening, but are they just conspiracy theories and delusional fantasy? Science-fiction? Or could any of it really be true?

***

Some involved in theorising what lies behind the cause of human disappearances believe it's possible that advanced technology is now being utilized in the snatching of people; technology honed by the skills of advanced scientific experimentation that has been furthered beyond anything we could imagine, making the abductions sleek, speedy, invisible, and impossible to stop.

Invisible drones capable of tracking and snatching someone, their presence undetectable through the use of cloaking technology, rendering them completely invisible.

A substantive amount of speculation has been made in terms of these scientific developments, and many believe it has been developed based on Tesla technology seized from him before his death.

Believers in this capability point to the number of patents on record that involve advanced 'weapons' systems developed for controlling people by the use of vibration, infrasound waves, nano and plasma technology.

Futurist Alfred Webre, a Yale educated attorney who has taught at Yale and worked at the Stanford Research Institute now runs the Exopolitics website and Radio Show.

He claims that DARPA (Defence Advanced Research Projects Agency) and the CIA are in possession of secret time travel technology, and says that thousands of innocent people have been used by them in their experiments, resulting in their deaths or disappearances.

He says they have had Tesla-based quantum access time travel technology for nearly fifty years and it has been 'weaponized' for uses such as control over humans, surveillance, and "psychotronics."

Physicist Dr Elizabeth Rauscher once studied the effects of electro-magnetic weapons on people.

"Images can be impressed onto the mind without visuals," she revealed as far back as the early 1980's.

In other words, people can be made to see things that are not really there.

Silent Sound waves sent by distance at very low frequency can induce fear, panic, or suicidal thoughts. Psychotronic weapons can allegedly cause illness or even death at a distance.

Silent and invisible tools of covert attack. Neuro-weapons, Mind-control weapons, Directed energy weapons. Electromagnetic weapons. Smaller, personalised versions of HAARP and Chemtrails. All of these allegedly able to negatively influence and attack a target from a distance.

Invisible, operating in stealth, disabling or killing, and leaving no trace.

"They operate at the speed of light," says Harlan Girard of the Institute of Science in Society, London.

Are there invisible drones capable of lifting a person and abducting them?

Can directed energy weapons simply vaporise someone?

It has to be said that this particular field of study is full of disinformation, conspiracy theories, hoaxes, and opposing beliefs; everything seemingly impossible to validate completely, yet all entirely possible, and there is evidence of it.

Chapter Ten:
The Work of Satanists?

The Jamison family; husband, wife and their six year old daughter headed out to the Latimer Mountains of Oklahoma looking for a new home to move to, on October 8th 2009.

After their family realised they had not returned, an enormous search party was organised with hundreds of volunteers, troopers from the Oklahoma Highway Patrol and agents from the FBI.

The searchers combed the area on foot, on ATV's and on horses but they found nothing; even with the sixteen teams of tracking dogs that had been used.

Then a few days later their truck was discovered by hunters. It was locked and inside it the family's dog was close to death. Investigators discovered the family's cell phones and a very large amount of cash. There were no tracks however to lead them to where the family could have gone.

The 31-year-old Sheriff, a former U.S. Army Ranger, said his mind was consumed by questions and theories.

"Throughout this whole process I've found myself going back and forth as to what might have happened," Israel Beauchamp said. "I'm at my wit's end. I asked for all the help I could get. FBI agents; private investigators who contacted me."

If it had been straight forward foul play, surely the perpetrators would have stolen the money; there was over $30,000 in cash in the vehicle.

A man who lived a quarter mile from where the pickup was found was the last known person to see them. He too was questioned. He saw no-one else in the vicinity.

Many have wondered were they drug users? Was it a drug deal gone bad? Others have wondered were they in the process of turning state's evidence against drug dealers?

Was it simply a criminal case, or was something much deeper to this?

As people in the area speculated and tried to understand what had happened to the family, an edition of *The Oklahoman* headlined the story. The mother of Sherilyn Jamison was telling the Newspaper that her daughter "was on a cult's hit list."

According to Oklahoma's *Red Dirt News*, husband Bobby had allegedly been reading a "Satanic Bible" and had asked a Church Minister how he could obtain "special bullets" that would enable him to kill the demons that were terrorizing the family.

Security camera footage recorded at their home, installed by the family due to their concerns of the alleged spiritual attacks they were complaining of. It shows both adults walking around at times in a trance-like states and disorientation prior to their departure.

Approximately a month before the disappearance of the family, local Pastor Carol Daniels was found horrifically murdered in her Church nearby. The local D.A. Mr Burns said of the crime scene that it was "the most horrific he'd ever seen," but he wouldn't go into details as to why. Her mutilated body though was found behind the Church Altar in a crucifix pose, obviously suggesting a link to Satanic ritual.

Then in November 2013 bodies of two adults and a child were found by a deer hunter about four miles from their truck. It was believed to be the skeletal remnants of the family.

This was odd because the Jamison father could not walk more than a few metres without experiencing severe pain, and Cherylin had chronic pain in her neck and shoulder. Both were on disability, yet they were found on the opposite side of the low mountain area where they'd left their truck.

Their 'abduction' has echoes of eerily similar unexplained missing person's cases that have been documented over the last couple of centuries; the 'abduction' takes place in a remote wilderness area with dense or difficult terrain.

The 'abductors' one assumes, must have had the ability to not only control and transport these people from their truck through rugged terrain; they also left no other vehicle tracks, nor footprints, nor scent.

While the Jamison's fate may simply be a case of human intervention, *Reddirt news* make a point of the synchronicity that both the area where their bodies were found, and the site of the Church where the pastor was murdered fall on the 'Occult line of tragedy;' on the 33rd parallel north.

Occultists see the number 33 as containing the highest of sacred power. Occult scholars and conspiracists claim that the Illuminati and the 'power elite' have staged murders on or near the 33rd parallel north throughout history.

In Occult belief, sacrificial rites enacted at the 33rd parallel have far more power than any other geographical locations. 33 is the satanic number of completion, and holds the power of transmutation.

According to expert Occultists and conspiracists alike, including the late occult researcher John Downard, it's the 'kill number;' and the murders carried out are for a ritual called the 'Killing of the Kings' where the life-force is believed to be passed from the victim at the point of death to those carrying out the ritual.

They point to the grand events of the Hiroshima atom bomb, the JFK assassination, and the bombing of Babylon in the Iraq War, as all being planned along this sacred line.

Curiously, there was a similar case in 2013 in Eufaula, the Jamison's home town. Thirty year old Native American Tommy Eastep vanished on his return journey after spending a July 4th weekend trip there visiting his family. His truck was found abandoned on September 29th, in a rural area north of Holdenville; his keys, credit card and driver's license locked inside.

According to his older brother Clint, talking on blog talk radio, it was a good four miles off the main highway on a county road more like a cattle road. He says, "It was parked as deep as you could go. It probably stopped because there was overhanging tree and the truck couldn't go any further. There's a lake nearby, lots of small ponds around, and a large heavily-wooded area to the south and west.

Clint says, "He was a family man. He had kids. He wasn't in any type of turmoil, you know, that he walked off without his license, his debit card, his keys, his vehicle, and his belongings. He did not walk away."

Despite tracker dogs searching throughout the area his truck was found in, no trace of him has been found still. There is no suggestion here of occult intervention, although again his abandoned vehicle was found at a cross roads on the same symbolic degree of latitude.

Returning to the Jamison family, some sources including Discovery TV state that the tracker dogs *did* trace their scent, to a water tank near where their vehicle was found. This was an indication that their bodies had likely been placed inside the water tank, but when it was emptied they were not found.

Were they killed in the water? They were found almost three miles away with no tracks and both were partially disabled and unlikley to have walked that far voluntarily. Despite the search radius being extensive, they were not found during all the searches. Where had they been? Were they being kept somewhere? Were they kept in the water tower?

This theory of the Jamisons deaths perhaps ties-in with the ritual motive when looked at other similar cases. The most comprehensive investigator into remote disappearances, David Paulides of the Missing 411 series of books, which lists hundreds of inexplicable disappearances, has pointed out that many of the cases he's covered involve bodies being found in or near water. Then there's also the unusually large number of college males disovered dead in water across many US States, as documented by journalist Kristy Piehl, initially dubbed 'The Smiley Face Killers.'

Since the mid '90's, scores of college age men have been vanishing without trace to be found weeks or months laster in rivers or creeks in areas search parties have thoroughly seached several times before.

Often it looks as though their bodies were placed there to be found. Piehl first brought these strange disappearances and deaths to light when investigating one of the deaths of the missing men and after being contacted by two retired police detectvies, Kevin Gannon and Anthony Duarte who'd discovered many more similar inexplicable deaths.

Listing just a couple of the cases here, Chris Jenkins was found four months after he disappeared one night in 2003. His death was first deemed an accidental fall into the river and subsequent drowning, even though he was on the college Swim Team at Minnesota University. His body was found encased in ice with his hands folded over his chest in a manner that was wholly inconsistent with drowning.

Jared Dion was disovered in a Wisconsin River in 2004, five days after he'd disappeared. The coroner ruled he had not been dead any longer than 72 hours; that left 2 days unnaccounted for, which implied that he had been kept somewhere and placed in the water later.

Todd Geib was last seen in June 2005. When he was discovered in a remote bed of water his death was ruled as drowning, however when a new autopsy was carried out he was discovered to have been dead for only 2-5 days despite being missing for more than 3 weeks. Again, he had been somewhere else, alive, for approximately 2 weeks prior to his death. Where he was found had been thoroughly searched at least 3 times.

Chillingly Piehl has counted over 100 similar cases; all young men, all actively fit and often even on the Swim Team. Some will say they were drunk and fell in the water, but for anyone looking into the cases, it's hard to believe this is what really happenened.

Professor Gilbertson at St Cloud University, talking about one of the cases, has stated that the victim's blood was completely drained from his body prior to him being found.

The two detectives think it's got to be more than one killer. Bodies have been found in different States at the same time.

Gannon says of one victim, "He was stalked, adbucted, held somewhere for an extended time, murdered and disposed of."

It's been reported that sometimes it looks like the victim's clothes have been removed and put back on them, their I.D.'s always left on them but any religious jewellery they were wearing has been taken.

Jerry Snyder, former DEA and now founder of not-for-profit group Find Me, has studied more than 200 cases across the Country.

"We think we've only scratched the surface; that's what's really scary to me," he says.

Is it a gang of serial killers? A syndicate of some kind? Why is religious jewellery taken and their bodies often posed in the water?

There are several theories being put forward by many interested in the cases, one of which points to the possibility of their deaths being ritual sacrifices, again thought to be based on the ancient alchemy ritual of 'Killing of the Kings,' where the victim's life-force energy is said to be passed to the occult murder(s) at the moment of death, supposedly giving them greater power.

In alchemy ritual a solid substance is said to be 'disolved' in water in a 'slow and silent operation.'

Could this really be what is happening? Is some kind of elite group conducting ancient rituals to further enhance their desire for power?

Adding to the water ritual theory is also the very odd case of Elisa Lam, whose death features a water tower; only in her case she was found dead in the water, unlike the Jamison family, who it can be suggested had been placed in the water and then removed.

This time the water tank was on the rooftop of a hotel. Partly captured on film is the shocking and mysterious death of Elisa Lam.

In June 2013, investigators ruled her death as 'accidental.' Several important questions however have failed to be answered. One of which is, why did she climb over fifteen feet up into a water tower on the roof of a hotel to get inside it? Another would be, what exactly was happening to her in the security footage of her in the hotel lift prior to her disappearance?

The twenty one year old Canadian student was staying at a cheap hotel in downtown Los Angeles while travelling on her own, taking some time out from college. She was found naked in the water tower, having been dead for two weeks. She was last seen on the CCTV camera in the lift, sometime before she ended up in the water tower. The parts in between are a mystery, but so too is what's happening to her in the lift.

Able to be watched on YouTube, the footage is difficult to comprehend and very eerie to watch. There is something very wrong going on.

She is seen entering the lift and pressing lots of the buttons quickly, then peeking out of the open door several times while she waits for the lift to close. It's almost as though she is fearful that someone is after her. Looking along the corridors, she waits as the lift door fail to close. Becoming increasingly distressed, she's seen making odd gestures with her hands, stepping out of the lift and hiding in the corridor, seeming to be terrified yet not fleeing the scene.

Is her imagination playing tricks with her? Is her killer there out of sight of the CCTV, but lurking within inches of her, waiting to abduct her? Is there something otherworldly about what is happening?

Some people studying the tape have implied there are strange shadows and movement seen inside the lift; shadowy movement, and even face-type forms appearing on the walls of the lift. Is this merely poor video quality and over-active imaginations, or was there something unidentifiable and supernatural manifesting in the lift with her?

At one point, she is seen waving her hands around in front of her, as though trying to feel for what is touching her and talking to her, that she cannot see. When she realises there is an intangible, invisible entity inside the lift with her, her horror grows and she becomes terrified, wrenching her hands together and bending her knees in fright, trying to maintain her grip on sanity when she does not understand what is happening to her.

Her behaviour is one of disorientation, fear, helplessness and shock. Some will say she was on drugs but none were found in her system. Others will say she was having a break-down but the tragic case has fascinated many and there are some incredible theories going around. Some strongly believe she was about to be attacked by something unseen.

Others feel her strange behaviour points to demonic possession and that she was clearly hearing voices. There's also the theory that she may have she died in an occult ritual; that she was used as a sacrifice, hinting at her name and the likeness to Aleister Crowley's poem 'Jephtha,' written when he was staying at the Cecil Hotel in London, the same name as the hotel in which she died.

They have pointed out that the poem has the line 'Be seen in some high lonely Tower.' In the poem, 'Jeptha' was a judge in the *Pseudo-Philo* works, (an ancient biblical text) who offered his daughter as a willing sacrifice. The girl is called Seila; an anagram of Elisa.

A coincidence perhaps? A conspiracy too far?

89

Others have speculated that she had been wanting to commit suicide. The hotel itself has an unsettling history of murder which may perhaps have left some kind of supernatural imprint on the building; its malevolent aura urging people on to commit acts of murder there. There are records of two serial killers having lived at the hotel. The hotel has also had an unusually high number of suicides.

However, there were far easier ways to do it. Was it even possible to get into the water tank of her own accord? There was no ladder there.

Is this all hysteria and speculation? Was she simply trying to get an old tempremental lift to move, by getting in and out of it and pressing all of the buttons, trying to see which one would get it moving?

But why does the security tape look like she's talking to someone who is not visible and reaching her hands out and grapsing the empty space in front of her as though trying to feel for something invisble that is right in front of her but that she cannot see. What is making her so distressed and confused?

Adding to the mystery is Dr Douglas James Cottrell, PhD. A highly regarded Canadian medical intuitive who claims he, like his predecessor Edgar Cayce, can access the Akashic Hall of Records. Through this he has given thousands of personal readings to people regarding their health problems, accessing their undiagnosed illnesses through a form of 'remote viewing.'

A former skeptic himself, it was when his child was born with a serious illness that he sought help with the diagnosis and through this journey met others like him who could help heal people. He undergoes deep meditative states to look into the past and the future, and is believed to be able to make accurate predictions and see what happened in past events. In one session available on YouTube, he relates what he 'sees' as having happened to Elisa Lam in the lift and up on the roof of the hotel.

He alleges that she was hearing voices in her head; but this was not from a psychotic breakdown, and it was not a demon. The voices were being 'beamed' into her head. They were calling her name, beckoning her; she was looking for the source of the voices and could not understand why she couldn't see the person or people around her when the voices were so close.

They were high pitched and uncomfortable, they were causing her distress, disorientation and fear. She was obeying the voices, going to where they were beckoning her so that she could find them. They led her to the water tower, says Dr Cottrell. They led her to her death and when she got to the roof he alleges, in his meditative trance state, there were pains in her head as though someone was pointing a laser beam at her head. Self-destructive thoughts were being given to her through the sound waves being sent through this 'laser' he claims.

Chillingly he says he can see a dark figure on the roof; cloaked in dark shiny clothing, a shadowed figure with its head covered by a balaclava or hood. He thinks it's a man but he also says it's possible it's a *discarnate* entity.

Others point to her online activity. Was a tweet allegedly sent from Elisa's twitter account really hers? There's the claim that from her twitter account, before her stay in the hotel, she tweeted a post about a Canadian company being given funding from the US for developing a 'quantum stealth' type of camouflage for soldiers that makes them invisible. The gear blends light around the wearer/ or an object, to create the illusion of invisibility. In that respect, a soldier, or anyone using it, can render themselves invisible to everyone else.

Has the development of cloaking technology created invisible predators that the unsuspecting person is powerless to see coming? Are people being silently snatched by something human but invisible?

These wild ideas and speculations could all be a range of conspiracy theories that have gone way too far, but perhaps not.

In Northern Ireland lies Ballyboley Forest, where mysterious stone formations and circular trenches are embedded in the ground, giving rise to beliefs that it's an ancient Druid site and a gateway to "the Otherworld," according to the Celtic tradition.

Although forest workers of the Park Service maintain the landscaped trails for visitors to use, there are other natural paths that never seem to need maintenance, that stay oddly clear of any foliage or branches, their paths always mysteriously remaining clear. It's said that the local people do not like to venture into the forest.

People who do enter it often return describing the eerie feeling that they were being watched. Tales abound of seeing shadowy figures standing amongst the trees, cloaked in brown robes, their heads covered. Ancient texts tell of mysterious disappearances of people who never returned from the forest.

In 2006, a man's body was found in the forest. The Police had issued an alert after he'd been reported missing since leaving his place of work two days prior to this.

The following day his car had been found at the edge of the Forest and the police had started to search inside it.

It was ruled that the man, Ian Black, from the nearby town, had died of natural causes.

One has to ask how it's possible to die of natural causes in two days in mild summer temperatures? It was not hot enough or cold enough to have succumbed to the elements.

In 1994, newspapers reported the strange incident of a couple who were walking through the forest when they suddenly heard screaming. Moments later a 'large dark shadow' appeared in front of them making them run off in terrror.

In 1997 two men reportedly said they were walking through the forest when they heard a flapping sound that was very loud. They didn't know what it was so tried to ignore it and carried on walking.

Moments later they started hearing what sounded like a woman crying and moaning in pain or distress. Cocerned for her state of health, they quickly tried to find her but could see no-one nearby.

What they did see however were trees smeared with blood all around them.

Running in fear, as they fled they both glanced behind them and to their horror both believed they could see a group of figures in dark cloaks standing where the trees were.

* * *

In Italy in 2006, it was announced that the police were to set up a 'Satanic Squad' to deal with the growing violence of Satanists.

It was to include not only policemen, but also priests that were expert in the realm of the occult. It came as a response to the rise in the number of horrific murders being carried out by Satanists. In one case, an occult group calling themselves 'The beasts of Satan,' had beaten and buried alive two of their own group deep in the forest.

* * *

In Russia in 2008, four teenagers went missing from their homes. For weeks, police searched for them, at a loss as to what could have happened to them.

Three months later, a gruesome discovery was made in the local woods. The remains of their bodies were found. They had been mutilated and burnt.

The police were able to identify one common link between them – they had all had telephone contact with a local boy by the name of Nikolai Ogolobyak prior to their disappearances.

Scientific and trial evidence later found that Nikolai, along with others, had carried out a sacrificial ritual of these young people. Each had precisely 666 wounds to their bodies, they had been scalped before being 'roasted' on the fire and some of their body parts eaten by the group, who proclaimed themselves Satanists.

The killers had marked the site in the woods with an upside-down cross.

Chapter Eleven:
More Mysterious Disappearances

Former Marine and Special Forces member, Robert Springfield, disappeared while hunting with his son in the Bighorn Mountains in Montana in 2004, in an area he grew up exploring.

Searchers combed the area for him, using a helicopter with infrared sensor, two dozen trained dogs, and over two hundred volunteers, but found no sign of him. Several thorough searches for him were undertaken. They came back again during the spring and again found nothing.

Then just over a year later, skeletal remains were found by hunters, along with the wallet and I.D. of Mr Springfield, oddly, say his family, in an area that was only fifty yards from where they had camped whilst looking for him in the search. The family are adamant that searchers had gone over the exact spot where his body was found. For this reason, they wondered, had he been killed and his body placed there later?

"If he was actually up there in that area, we would have smelled something," his wife said to Indian Country Today. "The animals would have been there."

His cause of death was ruled as 'undetermined.' His wallet was found with his remains. Inside were his ID and Social Security card. When they were given back to the family, there were no signs of any weathering or damage from rain to these items. This, the family believes, means they were not exposed to the elements for any period of time.

The disturbing implication here is that this would surely mean he was not in the outdoors the eleven months he was missing.

The family are understandably seeking explanations and some kind of justice and closure on this tragic and concerning case.

* * *

In Canada, there's a highway that has long since been renamed 'The Highway of Tears,' after decades of local females disappearing along the remote and rural route.

With its stunning views and its mountain backdrop, Canada's Highway 16 is an incredibly scenic 500 kilometre road. However, since the 1960's, and still continuing today, it is estimated that over forty women have gone missing or sadly been found dead parallel to the road, in the depths of the forests.

Some of the missing women were found to have been the victims of serial killer Bobby Fowler, possibly as many as nine women. As to the remaining large number of women missing, their fates are still unknown. The police do not believe he was responsible for any more, yet they also have no clues as to what might have happened to them.

In May, 2011, Madison Scott vanished near Vanderhoof along the highway. She had been at a party in a camping area and her tent and car were left remaining, but she had disappeared without trace, and she is still missing. A reporter with the Vanderhoof Omineca Express said, from talking with her family and friends, "She had her head screwed on. We don't think she just wandered off drunk and fell into the lake. It is completely out of character."

* * *

Then in June 1995 in Arizona again, Newspapers reported on the odd disappearance of trucker Devin Williams. It apparently left the local police authorities completely baffled, and the public coming up with theories which included alien abduction.

He was a long distance truck driver from Kansas. He'd left with his eighteen wheeler fully-loaded and headed out on his journey. Along the main freeway in the National forest area of Buck Springs, off Interstate 40, he'd inexplicably turned into a remote forest road and started driving up it. It was not a short-cut route to anywhere but the forest itself, and certainly not on his route.

His boss said afterward, "Why he would have driven into a rugged area like that, I don't know. No one can figure out what happened."

His truck eventually got stuck on the narrow dirt road. He disembarked and walked away from the truck. Hikers nearby were witness to his odd and erratic behaviour. They asked him why he drove the truck there. They said he pointed to the truck and said, "I didn't; they did it."

They told how he was barefoot, and seemed disoriented as he "talked to a tree."

That was the last time anyone saw him. He then vanished without trace.

There was no-one else in the truck.

He was a happily married family man by all accounts, who was regularly drug tested by his employer as part of the condition of employment. No-one could find any hint of a reason as to why he would want to just disappear, taking nothing with him.

Repeated searches were carried out for him with K9's, and yet they could find no trace of where he'd gone.

Investigators also had no idea who "they" were.

Two years later, his skull was found not far away. Many felt, because of his reference to "they," that he was referring to alien entities.

Or were there other 'voices' that had told him to do it? If so, where did those voices come from?

Whatever was responsible, they were invisible to everyone else.

**

***

In Olympic National Park, government employee Mr Gilman went hiking in June 2006. After he didn't return, Rangers and volunteers searched the area for ten days after finding his car parked at a popular hiking area.

The search by land, air and in the rivers turned up no sign of him. Dogs were called in, an airplane with an infrared that can detect body heat was used, and they were to spend more than thousands of hours looking for him; all without success.

Searchers have found no sign of him.

"It's a mystery...no clues," said one of the rangers.

Relatives remained hopeful because of Gilman's military background. He'd been a paratrooper and had worked in Iraq. People believed his survival skills would aid him.
Four days earlier, Stephen "Mike" Mason also took a walk into the woods and disappeared without a trace, in the same area. His wife had dropped him at the Forks Camp in the Forest. Again, all efforts to find the man were made.

Masons wife says she's sure of only one thing about the disappearance of her husband. "He didn't walk out of there," she said.

* * *

Thirty seven year old Jeanne Hesselschwerdt was vacationing with her long term boyfriend in Yosemite National Park in 1995 when they stopped their car at a popular parking point along Glacier Point road and got out to stretch their legs. They wandered through a wooded area and became separated.

After losing sight of her, her partner walked back to the spot he had last seen her at, and then back to the car, looking for her as he did so, but thinking she would be back at the car. When he didn't see her there he began to get concerned and on spotting a nearby Ranger, he asked for help to find her.

A search was launched within forty five minutes; which was to last for an entire week. Teams of bloodhounds were used, two helicopters, and hundreds of people spreading out to search far wider an area than they believed she could have covered in her disappearance, just in case.

An animal attack was ruled out by a park spokesman, saying there had been no fatalities or attacks reported in years. In the subsequent report by China Lake Mountain Rescue, who assisted, rangers called out to her during the initial search, and to each other, 'to establish that voice contact could be made over a large area.' In other words, as the searchers had called to her during the hours of her being missing, she would have been able to hear them and thereby respond.

She was not found.

Although there was a small suspicion that her boyfriend could have been responsible because no-one else reported sighting her, he passed a lie detector test easily and was completely exonerated with no evidence of there being any foul play.

The police and searchers were completely mystified as to how she could have completely disappeared in so short a time, without a trace. They were unable to positively identify any prints as so many of the prints they found looked the same as the searchers own prints, wearing similar boots as the lost woman.

The missing woman's sister-in-law Janet called it, "the most baffling thing."

Three months later, two men who'd gone fishing spotted a body in a stream. It was positively identified as that of Jeanne. It was three miles from where she had been last seen.

Talking to the San Francisco Gate news, one of the men, a Mr Ulawski, who was a local resident near the park, said that the location she had gone to was 'inaccessible to almost everyone except mountain climbers.'

If that is the case, the questions have to be asked, how and why had she got there? It is very possible to get quickly lost, disoriented and start to panic within a few moments of realising you are lost in such wilderness; but why would you then attempt to orient the most difficult terrain around you rather than seek a trail and the road, knowing you had not climbed rocks to get to where you were?

How she got to her location remains to this day a baffling mystery.

* * *

In September 2008 searchers began looking through a part of mountain forest for a missing man in the Adirondacks mountain region.

Jeremy Quinn, 38, had been reported missing at about 8 p.m. The search began as night fell and continued the next day. Quinn was a volunteer fire-fighter and caretaker for several camps in the area. He had last been seen at 7am that morning, saying he planned to check on a seasonal home before reporting in to his work head office; but he never showed up there.

His truck was found near the camp the following evening.

"He was born and raised here; he is very familiar with the land," Forest Ranger Capt. John Streiff said.

Forest rangers, sheriffs, and fire-fighters were combing the woods. An intensive Type 3 search was instigated, involving walking in a close-knit grid where each searcher can see the next searcher's feet. The Teams of volunteers walked the ditches, and scoured the landscape for miles around the command centre. Canine units worked the ravines, but they were unable to pick up a trace, and searches found no evidence of his whereabouts.

Nine days later, another caretaker found his body at the bottom of a cliff, a mile from where his pickup truck was found, and outside of the original search area. Police said they do not know how or why he had got from the truck to the cliff.

They ruled out suicide and there was no evidence of alcohol involvement, or foul play, they said. There were no signs of any kind of struggle or scuffle at the scene. They determined that Quinn died of multiple injuries resulting from a fall.

Reporter George Earl covered the story for Adirondack daily news, describing the special public meeting held at the Town Hall. For many, the meeting seemed to create as many questions as it answered. The range of responses to the police explanation of what had happened included disbelief, bewilderment, and fear.

"It's puzzling to figure out how he got from where his truck was to where he was found," said his fellow volunteer fireman and rescue worker Ron Konowitz. "It's difficult to believe."

Residents asked why his body was found so far from his truck. "We have no idea what brought him to that area," the Sheriff in charge said.

"He said he was going to check on a camp for a minute and then ended up way there?" town resident Terry Gregory asked. "I just don't believe it. It's all just very strange."

Residents wanted to know why the dogs in the search were not able to track the man and why an extensive 150 person search had uncovered no footprints or any other evidence that he had walked to the cliff from his truck. There was no evidence at all indicating a path of travel between the two locations.

Friends, co-workers, along with the media, had too many unanswered questions; of how and why he came to be there. His truck, with the keys in it, a mile away; between the truck and his body lay a tangled forest and steep ravines. Why would he go through that?

Astonishingly, over three hundred people go missing or are injured each year in the Adirondacks alone. Though it is an incredibly rugged area and nature itself can be deadly, some of the cases of missing people are simply very strange to say the least.

In these last two cases, what would make both people go to the most inaccessible and dangerous parts of the area, with no reason at all to do so?

Both were not known by those close to them to have had any mental disorder, depression or other reasons to want to end their own lives, just like the earlier case of Devon Williams and yet, their behaviour seems out of the ordinary.

There are other very strange cases of incidents that also lack any reasonable explanation, yet those who have survived them have spoken of possible reasons.

For example, in Massachusetts is Freetown State Forest, and in the forest there is a ledge called The Assonet Ledge. It's said that there's an association with it being a place of sadness, of a feeling of being filled with dread on approaching it. Indeed, more than a dozen suicides have been recorded here; the visitor being overwhelmed with the sudden inexplicable need to jump off the ledge, to throw themselves over it into the deep quarry below, often in front of their companions.

The ledge consists of granite; the same stone as the foundation of a bridge in Overtoun, Scotland, where as many as fifty dogs have inexplicably jumped to their death from the bridge, in front of their owners, each time at the same spot.

Dr Sands, an animal psychologist was asked to go there to try to understand what was happening. He took a dog over the bridge and noticed that at a certain point, the point where all the other dogs had jumped, it tensed immediately. The only thing in view at this point is the granite of which the bridge is constructed. This has led some to wonder whether the granite is the real instigator of the phenomenon.

Granite is composed of quartz crystal. Crystal is a conductor used in computers, radios, and televisions for its conductive capabilities. It also has the amazing ability to store and hold memory.

Many in the paranormal investigative world believe the theory that quartz is a conductor for paranormal entities, enabling them to manifest more easily in this world through the quartz generator, and that paranormal energy is held in the quartz, never dispelling but remaining there afterward, never leaving.

It is true that spell casters traditionally use quartz crystals for spell casting, using the crystal to hold and intensify the power of their intent within it.

Another place which reputedly seems to lure people to their death is a natural pool in Babinda Boulders in Far North Queensland, Australia. It's called 'the devil's pool.' To the aboriginal people the pool is sacred, but it's a popular natural feature many wish to visit.

It's here that at least seventeen people, and many say more, have lost their lives in the pool. Some while swimming, but many others from the banks of the pool, with stories of people being mysteriously 'pulled in' by the water and ending up drowning in it.

There is also the case of teenager Andrew Green, who accompanied his father to an empty house in London that his father needed to inspect for his job as a housing officer. This was in 1944.

When Andrew reached the stairs inside that led up to a tower, he felt as though there were invisible hands on his back, pushing him up. On reaching the top of the stairs, he heard a deep voice in his head telling him the garden was only a few inches below him and that he wouldn't hurt himself if he jumped.

Andrew was only made aware of the deadly height of the drop when his dad suddenly grabbed hold of him and pulled him back from the edge.

Confused and disturbed by the incident, his father asked a friend of his who was a policeman to look into the history of the house, and to his shock it was discovered that there had been twenty suicides reported at that house, all of which involved the person throwing themselves off the tower where Andrew had been standing when he had heard the voice telling him to jump.

So perturbed by this experience Andrew went on to dedicate his life to studying the paranormal, strongly convinced he had been affected by a demon.

Through history there are a plethora of accounts of demonic attack, and the descriptions are remarkably the same. They toy with a person, get into their mind, and direct the most awful and destructive thoughts into their heads. They want to see the person destroy themselves and they aim to wear a person down until they are unable to defend themselves anymore. They are relentless, and will not stop. Their voice insistently telling a person to kill themselves.

Are all these accounts simply from those who are mentally ill? Or can demons attack even the most balanced of people?

* * *

Houston News in 2012 covered the baffling story of a trio of missing men in the Liberty County region; all their disappearances so far unsolved.

Speaking of the families, they said,

'The woods seem to have swallowed their fathers without leaving a trace.'

"How can people be swallowed and never seen again? This is crazy," said Kim, whose father Dennis was one of the three men to disappear months ago.

As she went around to local stores handing out pictures of her father made into fliers, the staff thought she'd already been there; it turned out instead that the fliers they'd already been given were for two other men already missing.

The men all disappeared within a few miles of each other. They were family men leading regular lives. Two of the men disappeared by the roadside after mysteriously abandoning their cars, leaving their keys inside the cars. Still the families and police have no clues.

Despite intensive searches by hundreds of people, infrared camera, taking dogs, and trained searchers, no trace of either of them has been uncovered, except for the coat of one of the men, Mark Rhineburger, found in a remote area several kilometres away. His daughter said that on the day her father abandoned his car, he had told staff at two garages that he was being chased.

Dennis Rogers vanished while taking his regular walk. His phone was traced by the nearest cell phone tower to miles inside a swamp. Footprints found which could have been his, went round in circles, but there was no sign of him.

Of the other man, Edwin Rogers, who also abandoned his car on the main road, no trace has been found and yet his family say he was unable to walk very far at all due to old injuries from military service.

Currently there are said to be forty missing person's cases in the two counties of Liberty and Montgomery alone.

Conclusion

Invisible, undetectable, and it leaves no trace. You can't see it coming and as much as you might try, you can't run from it.

The disappearances just keep continuing. There is no one answer; only some very disturbing possibilities.

This is a puzzle. An often deadly one. But perhaps some of the possible perpetrators have now been identified.

Or perhaps the mystery remains as one of the most enigmatic and perplexing of all time.

***

If you have experienced something strange and unusual like this, that's hard to explain, please feel free to let me know. I'm actively continuing to research and would be very interested.

Stephenyoungauthor@hotmail.com

Facebook; Stephen Young Author

Also by Stephen Young

Predators in the Woods

True Stories of Real Time Travelers

Encounters with the Unknown

Demons: True Stories of Demonic Possessions & Demon attacks.

Demons, Death & Murder. True Stories of Demons and the games they play

Made in the USA
Middletown, DE
06 January 2022